D1231811

Who Was
Joan of Arc?

Who Was
Joan of Arc?

by Pam Pollack and Meg Belviso

illustrated by Andrew Thomson

Grosset & Dunlap
An Imprint of Penguin Random House

To Anne Swain, Fearless Leader—PP

To everyone at *Angels on Earth*—MB

For Rhia—AT

GROSSET & DUNLAP
Penguin Young Readers Group
An Imprint of Penguin Random House LLC

Text copyright © 2016 by Pam Pollack and Meg Belviso. Illustrations copyright © 2016 by Penguin Random House LLC. All rights reserved. Published by Grosset & Dunlap, an imprint of Penguin Random House LLC, 345 Hudson Street, New York, New York 10014. GROSSET & DUNLAP is a trademark of Penguin Random House LLC. Printed in the USA.

Library of Congress Cataloging-in-Publication Data is available.

ISBN 978-0-448-48304-7   10 9 8 7 6 5 4 3 2 1

Contents

Who Was Joan of Arc?

English soldiers surrounded the great walls of Orléans (say: OR-lee-on), France. The people had been trapped inside the town without food for seven months. The English hoped that if they closed off the city long enough, the French citizens would open their gates and surrender.

France and England had been at war for as long as the people of Orléans could remember. The Duke of Orléans, the town's leader, had already been captured by the English. His half brother, John de Dunois, did his best to defend the town. But he couldn't drive the English away. The people of Orléans were beginning to lose hope. They were hungry. They thought of another siege ten years before in another French town. It had lasted a full year. The people of that city had been forced to eat cats, horses, and rats to survive.

Eventually that city had surrendered. The people of Orléans didn't want to surrender, but what else could they do? "We need a miracle," they said to one another.

And maybe a miracle was coming! People who managed to sneak inside the gate of Orléans brought news of a very special peasant girl. She saw visions. She spoke to angels and saints. Her name was Joan of Arc. On April 29, 1429, the citizens of Orléans heard amazing news. Joan had arrived! She had slipped through an unguarded gate in the wall and entered the town. And she wasn't alone. She brought men who wanted to help, and wagonloads of food and farm animals. Hundreds of people ran to see her.

What they saw was a seventeen-year-old girl who wore her hair cut short and dressed like a boy. She wore a suit of armor specially made to fit her small frame. She carried a sword and a banner with angels on it. The banner read "Jhesus Maria" for Jesus and Mary. She was on a mission to save the town of Orléans.

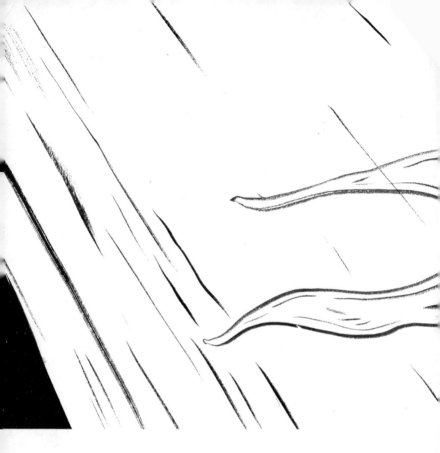

When the people of Orléans looked at Joan, they saw an unlikely hero who they believed had been sent by God. With her sword at her side and her banner raised high, Joan was a living symbol of hope for the people of Orléans—and for all of France.

CHAPTER 1
A Hundred Years of War

Joan of Arc was born in the village of Domrémy, France. It is believed that her birthday is January 6, 1412, but there is no official record. Her family called her Jehanne, but she eventually came to be known by the English form of her name: Joan. Joan's father was Jacques d'Arc. Her mother was named Isabelle. Joan had three older brothers, Jacquemin, Jean, and Pierre, and a sister, Catherine.

As a girl in Domrémy, Joan was taught to sew and spin wool into yarn. Joan, her brothers, and her sister carried water from the village well to the house, and they helped care for the family's cattle and sheep. Like many of the other children in the village, she never learned to read or write.

She dressed like an ordinary country girl of the time, in a simple dark red dress.

In the woods outside her village stood an old beech tree that was said to have once been the meeting spot for a fairy and the man she loved.

Villagers called it the fairy tree. In springtime, boys and girls hung flowers there and danced. They said the stream nearby was magic and could cure illness.

Whatever magic beliefs there were in Domrémy, the official religion was Roman Catholic—the people were Christians. Joan was a good Catholic. She prayed every day and went to church every Sunday.

Life in Domrémy should have been peaceful, but the country was torn apart by war. In 1420, when Joan was eight, the French king, Charles VI, signed an agreement with England's King Henry V.

It said that Henry's son—who was Charles's grandson—would rule both France and England. Many French people felt betrayed by the treaty. They did not want an English king—even one who was part French—to rule them. They believed their true king was Charles VI's own son Charles, whom they called the dauphin (say: doe-FAN). But not all French people liked the dauphin. Some wanted to be ruled by the English king. When Charles VI died in 1422, everyone fought over who was the true king.

Growing up, Joan saw many boys from Domrémy fight with boys from the neighboring towns over who should win the war and who should rule France.

One day in 1425, thirteen-year-old Joan was working in her family's garden. She heard someone speak her name. When she turned to see who it was, she saw only a bright light. Joan was terrified! She ran away. Not long after, the voice returned.

Hundred Years' War

In 1328, Charles IV, the king of France, died without any children to inherit his crown. The empty throne soon became a prize to fight over. The English king, Edward III, claimed that he should rule France because he was the nephew of the dead king. But the French chose a cousin of Charles

King Edward III

instead. England declared war on France, and the two countries would continue to fight on and off for decades. The Hundred Years' War, as it was called, lasted from 1337 to 1453.

By the third time she heard the voice, Joan was certain who it was: It was an angel. It was Michael, the archangel, who led God's armies in heaven. Saint Michael was considered to be the guardian angel of Domrémy.

In Joan's time, most people believed in angels. Visions from God did not seem so extraordinary. Joan didn't think she was imagining things. The archangel Michael continued to visit her. He told her to be a good girl, to go to church, and to obey her parents. Joan did her best. Soon the spirit of Saint Michael was joined by two others: Saint Margaret of Antioch and Saint Catherine of Alexandria.

Saint Margaret of Antioch   Saint Michael   Saint Catherine of Alexandria

When Joan was sixteen, the saints told her something new. She was destined to help the dauphin become king. Joan was stunned. How could she, a young girl, expect to help the prince of France? How could she win back his kingdom from an invading army? It seemed impossible. But Joan had strong faith. She believed in her visions. And she believed that with God's help, anything was possible.

The first problem was to figure out a way to meet the prince. She knew her parents would not let her leave home by herself. But as she said later, "Since God had commanded me to go, I must do it. And since God had commanded it, had I had a hundred fathers and a hundred mothers, I would have gone." She had never even been very far outside her own village. Joan was not sure *how* she was going to do it, but she was determined to save France.

CHAPTER 2
Leaving Home

In the summer of 1428, Domrémy was raided by the French soldiers who sided with England. Joan's family left to stay at an inn in a nearby town.

Joan thought that the French people who sided with England were betraying their country. Joan's visions told her that with her help, Charles, the dauphin, could drive the English out of France. Joan didn't understand what that help would be, but she trusted that her visions were true. At that time, the dauphin was in the town of Chinon, over 350 miles away.

Joan had a cousin who lived not far from the commander of a French fortress. Joan told her parents she wanted to visit her cousin, who was going to have a baby. What Joan really wanted was to speak to the commander—Robert de Baudricourt.

Robert de Baudricourt

When Joan arrived in December, her cousin's husband took her to meet Baudricourt. Joan explained that she needed to get to Charles. Like many Frenchmen, Baudricourt had heard of a prophecy—a prediction about the future— that a maid (an unmarried girl) would win France back from the English. Perhaps the maid was Joan! But Baudricourt was not so easily convinced. When Joan told him that God said that she would make Charles king of France, Baudricourt did not believe her.

He told Joan's escort to take her back to her father and have him punish her for telling stories.

But Joan did not go home. She remained in the town, determined to convince Baudricourt of the truth of her visions. She said, "I must be with the king . . . though I wear my legs to my knees on the road!" Joan meant that she didn't care how far she would have to walk to meet him. Like most poor people, she had never learned to ride a horse. The people of the town all heard about the girl in the red dress who claimed she was going to save France. One of these people was a young knight called Jean de Metz. He soon became her most loyal supporter.

Jean de Metz

Commander Baudricourt was surprised when Joan didn't give up. Eventually he was won over by her determination. He wrote to the dauphin about her. Amazingly, Charles agreed to a meeting.

Knights

A knight is a special soldier honored by a king or queen for his loyalty and bravery. Usually a knight worked in service of a lord, a man who owned land and a castle. Knights became known for following a code of chivalry. This meant they were expected to be brave and honorable and to protect those who couldn't protect themselves.

Knights often traveled with a personal servant, called a squire. Squires, archers, and foot soldiers might be killed if they were captured. Knights, on the other hand, were usually treated well and returned to their lords. Knights were known for being excellent horsemen and skilled fighters in battle.

News of the girl who talked to angels and was going to save France quickly spread. Joan was so confident about God's orders that people began to believe in her. They were thrilled when Charles said he would meet with her. That made Joan's mission seem even more real. If this poor girl had managed to get the dauphin's attention, what else could she do?

Before she left for Chinon, Joan told Baudricourt that she had received a new message from the saints. She told him the French army had been defeated that very day in a faraway city. Baudricourt was puzzled. The battle had taken place many miles away. No one could have heard the outcome yet.

In 1429, Joan left to meet with the dauphin. She traveled with Jean de Metz, his squire, an archer, and three servants. Crowds came to see them off at the city gate. In preparation for the 350-mile trip, Joan cut her long hair and changed her red dress for a boy's traveling clothes.

The saints had requested that she dress this way, even though it was considered very shocking for a girl to wear boys' clothes.

Days later, news of a French defeat reached Commander Baudricourt. Everything had happened just as Joan said it did. The voices Joan had been hearing seemed to know details that even important officials did not. This seemed to prove to Baudricourt that she really was being guided by God. But could Joan really predict the future?

CHAPTER 3
Sword and Banner

At first the soldiers who traveled with Joan and her knight, Metz, didn't know what to make of her. They were surprised to find themselves escorting a teenage girl to meet their prince. But the longer they traveled with her, the more they believed in her. It took eleven days for Joan and her friends to reach the castle fortress of Chinon.

When they arrived, they waited for the castle guards to let down the drawbridge so they could enter. One of the guards insulted Joan. She told him that someone dying so soon should not be so rude. Later in the day, that very guard drowned in the waters of the moat that surrounded the castle walls. Had Joan secretly known of this man's future?

Charles had heard all about Joan from Baudricourt. but he didn't yet know if he should trust her. So he decided on a test. Joan was led into the castle. She entered a room lit only by candles. It was filled with hundreds of knights. Only one man was dressed like a prince. But Joan walked right past him to another who was dressed plainly. He was short. He had a big nose and droopy eyes. Joan dropped to her knees before him and said, "Most noble dauphin, the king of heaven announces to you, by me, that you will be anointed and crowned king."

Joan had passed the test. She had known Charles even though she had never met him and even though he had been in disguise.

At the castle in Chinon, Joan met John, Duke of Alençon. He was only twenty-three, but he had already spent five years as an English prisoner. It didn't take long for him to pledge his loyalty to Joan. She called him her "Beau Duc," or "Handsome Duke."

Duke of Alençon

But not everyone was convinced by Joan. Charles was surrounded by counselors. Many were greedy and selfish and had their own plans. They demanded that priests talk to Joan to make sure she wasn't working for the devil. Joan was questioned for three weeks by the local bishop.

Sometimes Joan got impatient with all their questions and demands for signs proving that she was sent by God. "In the name of God, I did not come here to give signs," she said. "But take me to Orléans and I will show you the signs for which I was sent."

Finally Joan prepared to leave for Orléans. On March 22, 1429, Joan had someone write a letter for her and sent it to the English commanders, telling them to leave France on God's orders. The English army didn't respond. They simply captured the messenger, known as a herald, who had delivered the letter!

In order to free the town of Orléans, Joan would have to lead her soldiers into battle against the English. There were many things she needed to learn about warfare. Her many supporters had given her a horse that she had quickly learned to ride well. Now she needed a weapon—a sword.

A vision of Saint Catherine told Joan that she could find a sword hidden in a chapel a short distance away. It would be buried near the altar.

Joan sent a message to the priests of the chapel and asked them to find the sword for her. When the chapel was searched, the sword was just where Joan— and Saint Catherine—said it would be. But the sword was old and rusty. It didn't look like it could protect anyone in a battle. Miraculously, when one of the priests touched it, all the rust fell away.

The old sword was ready for battle!

Next, Joan had a suit of armor made. She predicted that she would be wounded at Orléans by an arrow above her chest, but not killed. Her armor was paid for by donations from the French people.

Saints

A saint is a person who has lived a very holy life and is thought to have a special relationship with God. In the Catholic faith, people often ask the saints to pray to God on their behalf. Only the pope—the leader of the Catholic Church—can declare someone a saint. Sometimes it takes centuries for church leaders to decide if a person is worthy of the title. They need to gather proof that the person has lived a holy life. And they look for proof that two miracles have happened after praying to that person since his or her death.

French craftsmen also made Joan a banner, or flag, to hold high for other soldiers to see. Some say her banner showed angels holding a lily. Others say it showed God holding the world with angels on either side. Whatever image was actually on the flag, Joan said, "I loved my banner forty times better than my sword."

Joan and her followers, including her brothers Jean and Pierre, were ready for battle. Leading an army of four thousand men, Joan arrived outside Orléans on April 29. Most of the city walls were guarded by the English, but at night Joan was able to sneak in through one unguarded bridge.

She brought two hundred soldiers with her as well as supplies for the people inside. The rest of Joan's army hid nearby, waiting to attack the English.

CHAPTER 4
Victory

Joan and two hundred of her soldiers were now inside the walls of Orléans. Soldiers were not known for polite behavior. But Joan's army was different. She insisted that the men use no bad language. They had to go to church. When girls came to the camp to flirt with the soldiers, Joan ordered them away. Some of the soldiers resented being bossed around by Joan.

The English lived in forts that they had built just outside the city walls. Sometimes Joan called out to them over the walls of the city with orders to leave France. They shouted back that they would burn her if they ever caught her.

On May 4, French troops fought against the English at Saint-Loup (say: SAN-LOO), a town about a mile away. Back in Orléans, Joan woke suddenly from a nap. She was sure that there was fighting going on and French blood was being spilled! She raced out to Saint-Loup. When the soldiers saw Joan riding toward them with her banner, they felt as if God was on their side. They summoned their courage and beat back the English soldiers. Victory!

Joan learned more English forces would be arriving soon. The next day, May 5, was a holy day. It was considered disrespectful to God to wage war on holy days. All the armies—both French and English—honored the church's holy days, so there would be no fighting that day. Joan wrote another letter to the English. She tied it to an arrow and shot it at them. "I would have sent you this letter in a more suitable manner," she wrote, "but . . . you have kept my herald."

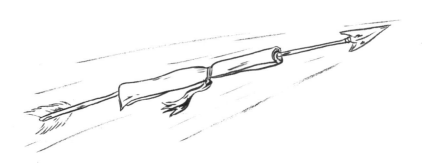

Joan offered to trade some prisoners for the herald, but the English only answered her with insults.

This brought Joan to tears—not because it hurt her feelings, but because she hated seeing so many people get hurt in battle. Joan herself had never—and would never—kill anyone. She didn't understand why the English didn't just go home to England!

On May 7, 1429, Joan set her sights on capturing two towers that stood on the outskirts of the city. English soldiers had been stationed in them. Joan and her French soldiers attacked the towers. Around noon, as Joan was climbing a ladder, she was shot by an arrow. The arrow went deep between her neck and shoulder. Her prediction about being wounded had come true.

Joan was carried away from the fighting by one of her loyal soldiers. It is said that she pulled the arrow out of her shoulder by herself. The shoulder was treated with olive oil and bacon fat to seal the wound. The French continued to fight, but it looked as if they would lose the battle until Joan—having prayed and rested—returned.

The sight of her banner waving once again gave the French courage. "All is yours!" Joan cried, touching her banner to the nearest tower. "Enter!"

The French were victorious. The next day the English retreated. The city of Orléans was now free. The townspeople held a parade to celebrate.

CHAPTER 5
Charles the King

Orléans was free. But Charles was still not king. To be king, he would have to be crowned at the cathedral in the town of Reims (say: RANZ). Joan and her soldiers set off for the city with Charles. Many towns lay between Orléans and Reims—and some of those towns were held by the English.

Joan and her French army captured one town after another that June. They seemed to be unstoppable. So Joan's soldiers were surprised when she told them to "have all good spurs." She meant the soldiers' horses would need to ride fast in this battle. Did Joan think they would need to run away from the enemy? No. She explained that it would be the English who ran. Joan's army would have to chase them. And that was exactly what happened.

On July 16, Joan and her army arrived at Reims, where Charles would be crowned. When she got there, she found her parents waiting for her.

They had come all the way from Domrémy to see the ceremony. The townspeople had heard all about Joan's victories against the English. They thought Joan was holy. They often asked her to touch and bless their personal possessions. Joan told everyone that her touch wasn't magic, but she was happy to touch the objects they brought to her.

On July 17, 1429, the dauphin was crowned King Charles VII at the cathedral. He was anointed—marked—with special oil. According to legend, the oil had come straight from heaven. This oil had been used to crown Clovis, the very first French king, and every king after him. By using this same oil for Charles, his followers hoped that no one could say he wasn't really the king.

Charles was crowned just like all the French kings before him—except for one thing. No other king had ever had a peasant girl stand beside him for all five hours of the ceremony. Joan brought her banner with her because "it had shared in the toil; it was just that it should share in the honor."

Joan made one request of the new king. She asked that her home town of Domrémy not have to pay taxes ever again. Charles agreed, and the town of Domrémy, France, paid no taxes for the next 360 years.

CHAPTER 6
Defeat

Charles VII was finally king. But the English still controlled many parts of France, including the capital city of Paris. Joan wanted to take back Paris for the French. She liked to make quick decisions and take action.

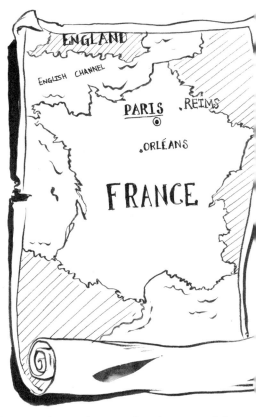

The king didn't like to do either. Charles would not let Joan go to Paris. Instead, he made a truce—

an agreement with the Duke of Burgundy, who supported the English. After fifteen days, the duke was supposed to hand Paris over to Charles. Secretly, Burgundy had no intention of doing this.

Duke of Burgundy

Joan had freed Orléans and gotten Charles crowned, just as the saints told her to do. She had completed her holy mission. But she couldn't bear to go home without being sure that France truly belonged to Charles. Joan knew that the duke was lying to the new king, so she decided to take her army to Paris on her own.

City Defenses

During the Middle Ages (around 500 to 1500) each town was its own fortress. The first line of defense against attackers was a wall. These took decades to build. They were usually made of a combination of earth and stone. City walls had large gates that let people come in and out of the city. At night, the gates would often be closed and locked. Sometimes a big ditch, called a moat, was dug outside the walls to keep out intruders. Moats were often filled with water, making it even harder for outsiders to gain access to the city.

After several weeks, Charles was finally convinced to take troops to Paris and help Joan win back the city for France. When the king arrived, Joan was waiting for him. The next day was September 8, a holy day. But Joan had waited so long, she thought just this once she would fight anyway. The battle started around noon.

In the evening, after many hours of fighting, Joan led her soldiers to one of the city gates. There they stopped to figure out the best way to cross the moat into Paris. Joan stuck a lance in the water to see how deep it was.

An English archer from inside the city walls took aim and shot at her. The arrow pierced her leg. Against Joan's wishes, the battle ended because of her injury. Even as she was carried from the field, she yelled that the city could have been taken.

The next day Joan was eager to start fighting again—only to learn that Charles had called off the battle. He had changed his mind yet again. It was hard for Joan to abandon Paris. Up until then, she had accomplished everything she had set out to do. Now, for the first time, she had failed.

Joan went to a nearby chapel where some of the soldiers wounded in battle left offerings to thank God for sparing their lives. Joan left her armor and her sword. She said, "I made an offering of a sword and armor. . . . That is the custom among soldiers when they are wounded."

Charles sent the army home. A writer said at the time, "And thus were the will of the Maid and King's army broken." He meant that in this moment, the French army seemed to have accepted defeat.

CHAPTER 7
Capture

Many of the soldiers in King Charles's army wanted to keep fighting. They hoped to capture even more French towns from the English. But Joan was ordered to do nothing. While waiting for instructions from Charles, she traveled with the king's court. Joan grew impatient. She didn't like waiting.

Over in England, in November 1429, the young son of England's Henry V was crowned king of France. Now there were two kings who believed they ruled France, one French and one English.

Charles VII declared Joan's family to be noble—a royal honor—and gave her a new last name: du Lys. The name meant "of the lily." He also gave them a coat of arms. But Joan continued to call herself the Maid. She didn't much care about being noble. She still just wanted to free France. She was not happy when Charles signed another truce with the duke that would last until Easter 1430.

In the spring of 1430, Joan was given permission to take her two brothers and a few hundred volunteers to capture a French town from the English. While on the road, during Easter week, she had a vision telling her that by Saint John's Day (June 24), she would be captured.

Coats of Arms

Coats of arms were pictures that identified important families. Knights wore them over their armor—*coat armory*—to protect and identify themselves. They were also used as a seal on important letters.

A coat of arms was made up of symbols that stood for ideas, such as bravery, that were important to a particular family. At first, men chose their own symbols, but some could be awarded only by the king. Joan's family's coat of arms had two fleurs-de-lis (lilies) and a sword holding up a crown, along with the motto *Vive Labeur* (Long live labor). Women weren't ever given coats of arms, so the fact that Joan's family received one from the king shows how special she was.

Fleur-de-lis

On her journey she stopped in a town to find the
people gathered around a statue of the Virgin
Mary, praying. They told Joan that a baby had
just been born who seemed to be dead. Could she
heal him?

Joan had told people over and over that she did not have special magic powers from God. She could not bless things or heal people. But she joined the others in praying for the baby. Suddenly the infant moved. He yawned three times. The baby lived for several days—just long enough to be baptized. Catholics at the time believed a person must be baptized in order to go to heaven. So these people believed Joan had saved the baby's soul.

On May 23, Joan and her men slipped into a town surrounded by English soldiers. Joan thought her troops could fight them off. When the English attacked, Joan rode out of the city walls to fight. The English were driven back to their camp. Joan and her men followed, chasing many of them far from the town. At that point, Joan and her men turned back to the city. Joan had led the chase after the English, but now she was behind everyone else, guarding the rear like a good captain would.

The governor of the town had been watching the fight from the city walls. Fearing that the remaining English soldiers would invade, he ordered that the city gates be shut once the French soldiers were safely inside. Some of the French soldiers—including Joan herself—did not make it in time. Joan fought hard against the English soldiers who surrounded her until an archer pulled her from her horse.

Some of her loyal men—including her brother Pierre—tried to save her, but couldn't.

The archer turned Joan over to his commander. At last the Maid had been captured.

She would never be free again.

CHAPTER 8
Prison

Joan was now in the hands of the Duke of Burgundy. The English wanted to put her on trial. But they were not the only ones who wanted Joan of Arc. Many important Frenchmen in the church didn't like Joan, because she talked to saints and angels without any help or permission from them. The Catholic Church was

willing to pay 6,000 francs for Joan, but the English king offered 10,000 for her capture. Only a king would be worth that big a

ransom. One person offered no money for Joan: King Charles VII, the very man she had been working so hard to defend and help!

While her enemies haggled over price, Joan was kept in a castle tower. She was afraid of what the English would do to her. She tried to escape by jumping out of a window sixty to eighty feet above the ground. Although she didn't get seriously hurt, she was found and returned to the tower.

The University of Paris

On November 21, 1430, the duke sold Joan for 10,000 francs to the English king. The church planned to hold a special trial, called an Inquisition, at the University of Paris to punish Joan for the crime of saying she had been sent by God.

Joan's trial would be held at Rouen (say: ROO-en), a French town that the English controlled. The English king of France, Henry VI, was living there at the time. He was only nine years old. The trial would be

Bishop
Pierre Cauchon

conducted by Pierre Cauchon, a French bishop who was loyal to the English.

Her own king, Charles VII, still did nothing to help Joan. Even though she served him so well, she got little in return. But Joan never stopped being loyal to the king.

The bishop made up a list of all Joan's crimes against the church—everything from sorcery (or witchcraft, the use of magic) to wearing men's clothes.

The Inquisition

In the twelfth century, the Catholic Church began holding trials to question and punish anyone they suspected of having beliefs that went against the church's teachings. Their targets included Jews, Muslims, and heretics—people who spoke out against the church and its teachings.

The person on trial was ordered to admit they were wrong. If they refused, they were tortured. The church had four major Inquisitions between the twelfth century and the mid-1800s: the Medieval, the Spanish, the Portuguese, and the Roman. Joan's trial was part of the Medieval Inquisition.

On December 23, 1430, Joan was thrown into the prison in Rouen to await her trial. She had five guards, three of whom stayed inside her cell with her. Her ankles were put in shackles, and she was chained to her bed. She might have been put into chains because people thought she had the power to fly away.

Since Joan was being tried for religious reasons, the law said she ought to be held in a church prison with nuns as her guards. Instead she was being held in a tower surrounded by male guards and soldiers who treated her roughly.

Joan's enemies, hoping to get evidence against her, even sent a man dressed as a priest to talk to her. As a faithful Catholic, Joan was grateful to be able to speak about her sins. But Joan was not a witch. She had not broken the law. So the spy had nothing to report.

On February 21, 1431, at eight in the morning, Joan of Arc entered the royal chapel in Rouen Castle. She was nineteen years old. The trial for her life was about to begin.

CHAPTER 9
On Trial

Bishop Cauchon was an important man in the church who had been to law school. Joan was just a poor farm girl. She couldn't read or write except her own name. She had never studied God or religion in school. She didn't even have her own lawyer to represent her. Cauchon didn't think Joan stood a chance against his Inquisition. He offered to let Joan choose someone in the court to defend her, but only her enemies were present.

Once Joan was facing him, the bishop discovered this peasant girl was a lot tougher than he had counted on.

Even though she'd spent months in prison, she was still strong. She still believed in her saints and in all the things she'd done for Charles VII.

The lead prosecutor—the man who would try to prove that Joan was a witch—yelled at Joan in the court and called her names. He tried to forbid her from praying.

The trial lasted from February 21 to May 23. The church did everything it could to prove that Joan was working with the devil. They brought up local customs in Domrémy like the fairy tree and tried to prove Joan believed in magic. One of Joan's worst crimes, as far as they were concerned, was that she dressed in men's clothing. They tried to convince her to put on a dress for the trial, but Joan felt safer dressed as a boy surrounded by male guards. She explained that she wouldn't change into women's clothing until the saints told her to.

The most dangerous questions for Joan were the ones about her faith. Bishop Cauchon hoped to trick her. He wanted her to say something that made it seem like she thought she was better than God. He wanted to prove she was lying. She was asked about the voices she heard and the visions she saw: What did the saints and angels look like? Did they have hair? Were they wearing clothes? What language did they speak?

Joan answered their questions directly. Sometimes she even made them seem silly. When asked if the archangel Michael was naked when he spoke to her, Joan said, "Do you think that God can't find him clothes?"

Sometimes Joan flat out refused to answer, because, she said, the saints and therefore God didn't allow it. Cauchon was furious at this young girl telling him that there were things that were none of his business. Once he ordered Joan to recite the Lord's Prayer. This was a test to see if she was a witch. He thought a witch would not be able to recite such holy words.

One day her questioners—agents of the church—asked Joan: Did she know if she was in the grace of God? This was a tricky question. They were asking Joan if she knew if God was pleased with

her and whether she would go to heaven. Both answers—yes or no—would be wrong. If she answered yes, Joan would be claiming to know things that only God could know, and that would show too much pride. If she said no, she would be admitting to being bad.

Joan gave an answer that avoided both traps. She said, "If I am not, may God place me there.

If I am, may God so keep me." Without a legal degree, Joan probably didn't know this was a trick question. But her simple, honest faith led her to an answer that stumped the clever judges.

As brave and strong as Joan was, the months of the trial took a toll on her. On April 16, 1431, Joan got very sick. The prosecutor went to see her in her cell and told her that her illness was her own fault.

Eventually Joan was well enough to go back for the next part of the trial, called "the Admonitions."

The church agents were going to pressure Joan to confess that she had been lying about talking to God.

On May 9, Joan was taken to the great tower of Rouen, where she was shown all the torture tools they would use if she didn't confess.

Joan was very afraid, but she didn't give in. She felt she had done nothing wrong. She had nothing to confess.

A couple days later, a very high-ranking Englishman left a dinner party with a few of his friends and stopped by her tower cell to make fun of her. Joan shouted back at them that the English would never take France.

For all her suffering, Joan was still holding strong. But her fate was in the hands of her judges, and when it came time to deliver a verdict, they found her guilty.

Medieval Torture

Those who would not admit to their crimes during the Inquisition were often tortured. Some of the most common—and horrible—forms of torture included:

- Dunking: In this popular test for witches, people were thrown into water. If victims floated, they were witches. If they drowned, they were innocent—but also dead.

- Freezing: Victims would be stripped, and freezing water was poured on them, usually in winter.

- Burning: Victims were either set on fire and killed, or slowly burned until they confessed.

CHAPTER 10
Saint Joan

On May 24, 1431, Joan was led to a cemetery where two wooden platforms had been built.

Surrounded by Bishop Cauchon and his agents, and crowds of English onlookers, she was told she was guilty of being a heretic, a liar, and a witch. They said that King Charles VII was also a heretic for believing in her. Joan told them not to say anything against her king, which made them furious.

The Inquisition judges asked her if she was ready to admit she had been wrong. Only by doing that would she save herself from being burned alive. "Do you want to be burned alive?" the judges asked. The crowd pressed forward, yelling, "Hurry up!" when she didn't answer.

At this moment, and for the first time, Joan lost her nerve. Faced with a horrible death, she signed a note promising to stop wearing men's clothes, to never fight in a war again, and to say the voices she heard were all a lie. Then Bishop Cauchon announced she would be imprisoned for life. He had her head shaved as punishment. Joan hoped that now she would finally be put in a church prison with nuns, but Cauchon sent her right back to the tower, this time wearing a dress.

Joan quickly regained her courage. Three days later she was back in men's clothes—perhaps because her guards themselves had stolen her dress to get her in trouble. Joan told Cauchon that the saints said she had done a terrible thing by signing the false confession. She took it all back. And in so doing, she condemned herself to death. She was only nineteen years old.

On May 30, at dawn, three doctors came to Joan's cell to tell her she would soon be burned to death. "I would rather be beheaded seven times than burned," Joan cried. When Cauchon himself appeared at her cell to walk her outside, Joan let him know she blamed him for her death. "Bishop, I die through you," she said.

Joan was dressed in a long black dress. She was led to a wooden cart. A pointed cap was put on her head. A sign on the hat described the crimes they believed she had committed.

English soldiers followed the cart through the streets to the platform where she would be burned. When Joan got on the platform, she fell to her knees to pray. She asked forgiveness of God and said she forgave everyone else. She asked people in the crowd to pray for her. Many of them burst into tears, even some of the men who had condemned her. Joan asked for a cross. She was given two sticks to make one. She kissed her cross and held it to her chest.

Not all of the English were moved by the scene. "Do you mean to have us dine here?" one called out to Cauchon. That was his way of saying, "Hurry up. We don't want to be here until dinnertime."

Joan was tied to a wooden stake, and the bonfire was lit from the bottom. Someone in the crowd held up a cross for Joan to look at. She was soon hidden by the flames, but she could be heard calling, "Jesus! Jesus!" One onlooker swore that when she died, a white dove flew out of her chest and up to heaven. Once the fire was out, her ashes were thrown into the Seine River.

One of the English cried out, "We have burned a saint!"

He turned out to be right. Twenty-two years later, in 1453, the English were driven out of France, just as Joan had predicted. Charles VII finally came to her defense and reopened her case. In 1456, the church reversed its decision and declared Joan innocent. The news was read out on the very spot where she had been burned. The notes of her original trial were torn up.

Over the following centuries, Joan's fame grew. People all over the world heard her story and came to love her—even in England. But nowhere was she loved more than in France. People began to talk of miracles that happened when they prayed to Joan. In 1920, she was declared a saint by the Catholic Church. Today, she is the patron saint of France—that means she is the spiritual guardian of the country.

Mont Saint-Michel (Saint Michael's Mount)

The Hundred Years' War continued after Joan's death. Off the coast of northwestern France, the English continually tried—and failed—to capture the island fortress of Mont Saint-Michel.

It was said that the Mont was built on the orders of the archangel Michael himself, and that he was guarding it with the help of Joan of Arc. A statue of Joan in full armor, with sword and shield, now stands on Mont Saint-Michel.

Every year on May 8, the city of Orléans still celebrates Joan's victory over the English.

She lived for only nineteen years, but in those years she showed more strength, courage, and faith than most. With no training or experience, she stood up to enemy soldiers, kings, and the powerful Inquisition at a trial that had already been decided against her. Yet her last words were to forgive everyone who had hurt her. She became one of the most beloved saints and a hero to even those who didn't share her religion or her nationality. She was proof that the poorest of peasant girls could be richest in faith and could save an entire country.

Timeline of Joan of Arc's Life

1412	Joan of Arc is born
1415	Henry V invades France
1420	Joan leaves home to help the dauphin become king
1422	King Henry V of England dies
	King Charles VI of France dies
1425	Joan hears voices for the first time
1429	Helps to free Orléans from the English
	Charles VII crowned king of France
1430	Captured by the English
1431	Her trial begins
	Executed by the English
1455	Her family petitions for a new trial to clear her name
1456	The Catholic Church overturns her guilty verdict
1920	The Catholic Church declares her a saint

Timeline of the World

1412	Eric of Pomerania becomes king of Norway, Denmark, and Sweden
1413	Henry V becomes king of England
1415	Pope Gregory XII resigns
1417	First use of street lighting recorded in London
1419	University of Rostock, the oldest university in Northern Europe, is established
1420	The Forbidden City is finished in Beijing, China
1421	North Sea floods what is now the Netherlands
1422	End of the Bulgarian Empire
1423	Death of Dick Whittington, former mayor of London, who inspired the English folktale "Dick Whittington and His Cat"
1427	First witch hunts begin in Switzerland
1428	The Aztec Empire wins control of Mexico
1429	Finnish city of Turku is destroyed by fire
1431	Vlad the Impaler is born

Bibliography

* Books for young readers

*Boutet de Monvel, Maurice. *Joan of Arc*. New York: Viking Press, 1980.

Brooks, Polly Schoyer. *Beyond the Myth: The Story of Joan of Arc*. Boston: Houghton Mifflin, 1999.

*Demi. *Joan of Arc*. Tarrytown, NY: Marshall Cavendish, 2011.

*Hodges, Margaret. *Joan of Arc: The Lily Maid*. New York: Holiday House, 1999.

Pernoud, Régine. *Joan of Arc: By Herself and Her Witnesses*. Lanham, MD: Scarborough House, 1994.

Pickels, Dwayne E. *Women of Achievement: Joan of Arc*. Philadelphia: Chelsea House Publishers, 2002.

*Poole, Josephine. *Joan of Arc*. New York: Alfred A. Knopf, 1998.

*Stanley, Diane. *Joan of Arc*. New York: Morrow Junior Books, 1998.

*Tompert, Ann. *Joan of Arc: Heroine of France*. Honesdale, PA: Boyds Mills Press, 2003.

Trask, Willard, ed. and trans. *Joan of Arc: In Her Own Words*. New York: Turtle Point Press, 1996.

*Wilkinson, Philip. *Joan of Arc: The Teenager Who Saved Her Nation*. Washington, DC: National Geographic Society, 2007.

Yeatts, Tabatha. *Joan of Arc: Heavenly Warrior*. New York: Sterling Publishing Company, 2009.

THE TIME-TRAVELING ADVENTURES OF THE ROBBINS TWINS

THE TREASURE CHEST

"Kids who have outgrown the
'Magic Treehouse' may enjoy this new series."
—*School Library Journal*

Join Felix and Maisie Robbins on their trips through time as they
meet thrilling historical figures as children in *New York Times*
Best-Selling author Ann Hood's *The Treasure Chest*!